Christian A. I

The keys to h

C. A. M. W.

Theoretical explanations

&

Practical applications

for the spiritual path of life

Christian A. M. Wagener

The

key

the

Hermeticism

Bibliographic information of the German National Library: The German National Library lists this publication in the German National Bibliography; detailed bibliographic data is available on the Internet at dnb.dnb.de.

© 2024 Christian A. M. Wagener

Publisher: BoD · Books on Demand GmbH, In de Tarpen 42, 22848 Norderstedt
Print: Libri Plureos GmbH, Friedensallee 273, 22763 Hamburg

ISBN: 978-3-7693-0808-2

Dedicated to a loved one.

Summary 6

Foreword and acknowledgements 7

Hermes Trismegistos the thrice great 19

Hermeticism and quantum physics 32

The hermetic seal of light 45

The principle of spirituality 51

The principle of correspondence 62

The principle of oscillation 74

The principle of polarity 84

The principle of rhythm 94

The principle of cause and effect 101

The principle of gender 111

Considerations! 118

Conclusion and S closing remarks 126

"To venture into the completely unknown,

I must enter it as I leave it:

As a traveller and alone"

Author unknown, AD 1917

Foreword

> *True hermetic transformation is spiritual.*
> Kybalion

Dear reader!

I have been involved with these many areas of esotericism for more than three decades. For me, the subject of magic/hermetics is an area of esotericism that has fascinated me the most to this day. But to really understand the things that are around you, it has always been important for me to learn from all areas of esotericism, borderline sciences and other subjects, such as psychology.

Some of you probably know me from my YouTube channel *Thoughts of Time* (as of 2023). There you can also find the video that inspired this book:

The Keys of Hermeticism & Sacred Geometry. It was from these thoughts that the idea for the book was born, although in a similar way, it has been kept in a drawer *unfinished* for a long time, to put it politely.

I am also reaching the age of 50.

It was time to take the book out of the drawer and combine it with the topic of hermetics. The main theme in this book was originally magic, which could be combined very well with hermetics.

From my point of view, an *alchemical* process increasingly developed, which came together when viewed as a whole.

You are holding the result in your hands today in the form of this book.

It was written down - forged - by me to the best of my knowledge and understanding.

I make no claim to absolute accuracy. Nevertheless, I was able to write this book with a clear conscience because it reflects my current state of knowledge and my personal truth.

Some of you have accompanied me through my YouTube channel over the years to this day. This book is my way of saying thank you and showing my appreciation for the support and trust you have always shown me.

If you don't know my YouTube channel *Thoughts of Time* yet, you are very welcome to have a look around, you are sure to find something useful for your spiritual path in life.

In addition, we can exchange ideas via the comments, which for me has always been a very important part of the YouTube channel. Let's stay with the foreword, which, despite the usual conventions, is different.

We are what we think. Everything we are comes from our thoughts. We shape the world with our thoughts.

Buddha

We know very well how much valuable **INFORMATION** can be contained in quotations. Even if we can't always decipher them straight away. The same applies to symbolism.

The quote I have chosen from Buddha is my absolute personal favourite, because it describes the structure of the **cosmos**, i.e. order, very precisely. Order, in turn, can only come about if it is subject to certain laws that are followed.

Because otherwise there would only be **chaos** - in other words, **nothingness**.

Both mirror each other on the same axis and yet are inversely different.

*But how do these laws come about that ultimately gave rise to our **universe** and thus to all of **existence**?*

We explore this question in this book. We use it to understand our spiritual **path in life** and walk it in **happiness**, **peace** and **love**.

That is why I would like to give you a key with this book, which is a useful tool to make our everyday life, our reality more pleasant, to experience and to understand!

In particular, I am convinced that the hermetic principles greatly enrich the spiritual path of life.

This book is of great personal value to me. If you study these topics of spirituality for so long, you should at least write a book about them to preserve the knowledge so that it is not forgotten, regardless of whether you publish it or not.

The information is retained!

As the first book on this variety of topics, this was the only choice I had to make and write for a long time.

The Keys of Hermeticism is a magical book.

There are seven principles of truth. The one who knows them, with full understanding, possesses the magic key at whose touch all the gates of the temple open.

Kybalion

Hermeticism is as old as the belief in magic itself. Regardless of whether it was known or not. Because the principles of hermeticism form the foundation of the entire cosmos.

Without these seven *principles*, also known as the seven *laws*, this reality would be inconceivable!

Spirituality is reconnecting with the natural sciences. This is an important step in the right direction.

Quantum theory shows that there are even higher laws than the previous understanding of our physics and our reality.

Hermeticism is not just a journey into oneself, but through the entire cosmos. In its most complete *form*, if I may call it that, it is the exploration of the whole of being.

The knowledge and understanding of hermetics brings about a clear sense of the natural order of the universe.

By understanding the 7 principles of hermetics, they can be applied not only to better understand one's own life path, but also to keep it in a positive, constant flow or to shift it.

These last three sections of text, which I have read, appear on the spine of the book in an abridged version, because they describe it aptly.

This book is deliberately short so that our thoughts and concentration are focussed on the essentials.

It facilitates repeated reading as well as the practical exercises of the 7 principles of hermetics in the applications.

This book is a guide and should be used like a workbook. For example, there are pages for your notes and thoughts.

I also recommend including one or two sentences in the focus of your consciousness, which one is that? - Trust your **intuition!**

I hope that this book fulfils its purpose for every reader. On the one hand, to give you a heartfelt thank you and on the other, to reveal to you, as well as to myself, further insights for our life's journey, your Chris.

Recognising more together!

The lips of wisdom are closed, but not to the ears of understanding.

Kybalion

Acknowledgement

For every good soul I have had the honour of meeting in my life.

Wherever the footsteps of the Master fall, the ears of those who are ready for his teachings open wide.

Kybalion

Hermes Trismegistos the thrice great

He is undoubtedly one of the *most* legendary people in history and is regarded as the author of the Hermetic writings and teachings. His most famous writing to this day is probably the Tabula Smaragdina. Better known as *The Emerald Tablets of Thoth the Atlantean.*

His name "Hermes" means something like "signpost" and comes from "herms". These were erected in ancient times as signposts or waymarks, the predecessors of which were simple piles of stones.

The name "*Trismegistos*" is a title and means:

The thrice great - The very greatest - The very great

According to ancient traditions, the name Trismegistos is synonymous *with "source of wisdom".*

The principles of hermetic teachings are deeply rooted in philosophical hermeticism or, to put it another way, hermetic philosophy.

The *Kybalion - The seven hermetic laws* are part of the learned writings that have only been passed on from master to disciple for a very, very long time. These collected and preserved writings were called *the Kybalion.*

The dialogue *Asclepius* from the *Corpus Hermeticum* is one of the best known of this work. Fragments of this dialogue were found in the Nag Hammadi writings that were discovered in a cave in 1945.

Hermeticism is also a way of life that is lived according to the seven principles. This is an essential point that is hardly or less mentioned in some recent books on hermetics.

Which I think is a great pity, because it is elementary!

By continuing to learn hermetics, the understanding of the cosmos and of oneself is expanded.

These insights are internalised and thus bring about TRANSFORMATION, i.e. the transformation or simply the transformation of the soul.

The hermeticist knows about such things and for him it is the *inner* alchemy - *the philosopher's stone*.

When we talk about hermetics, we are already in the realm of magic.

"Magic is the art of deliberately causing changes in consciousness"

Unfortunately, nowadays the term *magic* has been defamed and denigrated.

This has often resulted in very erroneous views of the true view of magic!

Back to Hermeticism. In 1593 in Venice, the hermetic writings of Hermes Trismegistos became better known to the public through the knowledge of masters and disciples. Since then, a line of personalities can be traced right up to the present day who have not only preserved this knowledge, but have also lived according to the seven principles.

In addition, the legend of Hermes Trismegistos can be traced back to ancient Egypt and even further. In Egyptian mythology, Thoth was the god of knowledge and wisdom, who was depicted as a human figure with an ibis head.

Thoth was also the patron saint of scientists, writers and magicians, although in my personal opinion the role in Christianity was and still is played by the archangel Uriel.

When the Greeks conquered the Egyptian empire, they worshipped Thoth as Hermes, the god of science and the art of rhetoric. Hermes was equated with

Thoth and the legend of Hermes Trismegistos began to take shape.

Hermes Trismegistos was also regarded as a *magician* and *alchemist* and is often referred to as the father and founder of alchemy.

Although there is no historical evidence for the existence of Hermes Trismegistos, his legend and his teachings are known worldwide, and not just since ancient times.

In many other cultures and civilisations on our planet, not only have the 7 principles of Hermeticism found harmony, but also the philosophical writings in particular.

In the Hermetic tradition, alchemy is understood as a spiritual transformation that is about transforming one's self into a higher self, this is the main reason for this book and the most sublime goal a Hermeticist can achieve!

Of course, it can be beneficial for every soul to transform negative qualities into positive ones, depending on their personal life path.

Traditional and philosophical Hermeticism has had a great influence on Western esotericism, including in the teachings of *Kabbalah*, *alchemy, magic* and also in some secret societies and orders.

Many of the principles of Hermeticism, such as the principle of *"as above, so below"*, have found their way into Western esotericism and have become part of the foundation and cornerstone of many spiritual traditions.

Through hermetics, the deeper study and meditation of the teachings and their spiritual practices, a connection to the higher levels of one's own consciousness can be established.

This inner alchemy is a process of inner transformation in which our soul/spirit is purified through the transformation of lower into higher forces.

Traditional Hermeticism is a profound and complex teaching that requires a serious and committed approach.

It takes time and effort to understand the deeper meaning and practical applications of hermetic principles and to apply them to yourself.

I am grateful to each of these precious spirits that this gift was and is not only passed on, but in particular that this knowledge was and is preserved and protected.

For me, as described earlier, the archangel Uriel is the patron saint of magicians. Because he has the same attributes as Thoth.

He shines his power and energy step by step for our spiritual path through life. He shines light on us in dark times and stages of life so that we can find our way back to the right path.

I have described this view, which is very personal to me, without touching on the religious aspect. Everyone must decide this for themselves. This is about the mystical view, which enables intuitive intuitions that are far removed from rational knowledge.

Intellectual judgement calls it intuition. My heart calls it a gift.

Over the years, I have learnt to put my trust in the gift.

Even if not every realisation was pleasant. Many things only become clearer afterwards that I have experienced myself, at least that was the case for me. Here and now, I am happy and grateful to be able to make my contribution to passing on and preserving the knowledge/key of hermetics.

In hermeticism, the universe is seen as a living, breathing being that is regulated by a higher intelligence.

This higher intelligence, I call it:

THE ORIGINAL SOURCE, is creator and preserver at the same time. I recommend the playlist "Die Urquelle - Die Suche nach dem Ursprung" from my YouTube channel *Gedanken der Zeit* for anyone who would like to delve deeper into this topic and my thoughts on it.

But I ask you to consider these videos as *experimental theosophy*.

Everything is connected to everything!

"Empty your mind, be formless, shapeless — like water. Now you put water in a cup, it becomes the cup; You put water into a bottle it becomes the bottle; You put it in a teapot it becomes the teapot. Now water can flow or it can crash. Be water, my friend."

Bruce Lee

The effect of this statement is that every action has an impact on the whole, always in proportion of course, but it is absolutely justified.

Every drop of water is connected to the sea!

Hermeticism and quantum physics

Here, too, we will start with a description before delving deeper into the topic. Because if we want to talk about hermetics and quantum physics, we also need to look at **Franz Bardon (* 1 December 1909 † 10 July 1958**. He was an occultist who had dedicated himself to *hermetic magic*. Here is a small extract from his book.

The path to becoming a true adept

"The transformation of one force into another is actually already an alchemical or magical process, but over time it has been generalised to such an extent that it is no longer regarded as alchemy or magic, but simply ascribed to physics".

If we compare the two areas in a short table, we can see at a glance that the **principle** is the same, just viewed from a different angle.

Hermetik/Magie	Quantenphysik
Durch Willen/Geist Materie beeinflussen!	Durch Beobachten (Messung) Materie beeinflussen!
Alles ist mit allem verbunden!	Durch Verschränkung identisch!
Viele Sphären/Ebenen vorhanden!	Quantenfeldtheorie! (vers. Felder)
Evokation/Beschwörungen	Frequenz/Dimensionswechsel
Heilenergie/Kraft	Quantenheilung
Hermetik/Magie ist höhere Physik	Quantenphysik ist höhere Physik

Let's take a closer look at the table to better understand the principle.

On the one hand, there is magic, which influences matter through **will/spirit**. In other words: **through our thoughts.**

Example: Will corresponds to the *element fire*, which in its *positive* form is constructive and preserving, and in its *negative* form has a destructive/decomposing effect.

All elements, including fire, arise from the ether principle, better known as Akasha.

This sphere, also known as the plane, is regarded as the cause principle.

This means that the entire being emerges and unfolds from this level!

Quantum physics!

In the double-slit experiment, particles of light, known as photons, are shot onto a kind of screen on which the arrival of the photons is registered. This results in an image made up of points of light.

Between the laser and the screen there is a partition wall with two columns that can be closed and opened independently of each other.

It is not possible to predict where the individual photon will land on the screen before this double slit is interposed, despite absolutely constant conditions.

Normal physics cannot answer this question.

"Chance decides where the individual photon lands!" Is the statement! - Unfortunately absolutely wrong!

"There is no such thing as coincidence!"

Just because the law is not understood or known, it is considered a coincidence.

I see it as a **probability wave** that interprets or defines itself through the calculation in *real time/pre-time* depending on the probability.

In physics, photons are considered to be both particles and waves.

Only during a measurement does the photon change its trajectory, its behaviour.

Our thoughts also have an influence!

Why don't we notice this in our everyday lives, which already changes the observation, the result?

Because measurements are taken constantly, every change is registered (stored) every change in air pressure etc.

In the simple words of the oracle from the film Matrix:

"One programme watches over the wind, another over the trees and the birds".

Every particle is subject to measurement, because the location, property and behaviour must be known at all times. Because this corresponds to an **order.**

In magic, we speak of the interaction of the elements.

"Everything is connected to everything"

As we have already read, this sentence comes from hermeticism/magic!

In quantum physics, this sentence remains true. There it is called *"entanglement"*.

Let's take a look at another experiment.

Entanglement means that two particles are connected to each other, even if they are spatially separated. A photon is shot through a lens and splits. Each particle takes its path in the other direction. If you now change the filter (polarity) of one photon, the other particle changes in the same way, without any loss of time - *spooky action at a distance.*

The questions that arise are as follows:

1. How does one photon know that the polarity of the other has changed?
2. Why does it have the same polarity?
3. How is the information transferred from one particle to the other?

The funny thing is that this realisation could already be the foundation stone for **beaming**.

To understand why the particles behave this way, we need to look at the table again and break down the next row.

Spheres/planes are well known in magic, they are even elementary. Each level has its own inhabitants. It is the same here on this plane that we inhabit, but that would be going too far off topic. For now, it is enough for us to know that we are on one of these levels. But not just on one level, because if you separate body, mind and soul, these levels are fanned out accordingly.

The **gross material plane** is the plane through which our body moves. This naturally applies to all living beings, such as humans, plants and animals, minerals, rocks, etc.. This level is dominated *by the element earth.* It is solid and solidifying.

The **mental sphere** is of a subtle nature and harbours our spirit. It also houses the **thoughts, ideas etc.** for our **consciousness.**

The **astral plane** is also called **the afterlife** because the astral matrix (soul) is located there! In other words, our consciousness. Because in the real sense, the soul is the connection to consciousness!

This level is not subject to time!

This is the only way to understand why the spirit/consciousness cannot pass, because time does not exist for consciousness, -

Therefore it is immortal!

It is also important to understand that we are not the thoughts. We are the consciousness that uses the thoughts!

All these described levels have different **degrees of density**, which gradually become more and more subtle.

However, it is important for us to understand that the astral plane also has different degrees of density!

Because the level of spiritual maturity determines which level we arrive at!

The description of the levels in their perfect form could fill books and requires intensive study! But it is enough for us to understand that when our spirit reaches a certain level, we are in that level accordingly. It is subject to the law of correspondence!

This implies that the only thing we are is consciousness, by degree of realisation. This realisation is decisive as to where our consciousness is located in the astral plane.

For here it should be enough to understand and it is not necessary to delve deeper to understand and apply this book and the use of the 7 principles of Hermeticism.

Nevertheless, I can recommend taking a closer look at this topic.

The hermetic seal of light

Hermeticism is also, as already mentioned, a way of life that is lived according to the 7 principles!

Through further learning of hermetics, the understanding of the cosmos and of oneself is expanded enormously. These insights are internalised and thus bring about TRANSMUTATION, i.e. the transformation or transmutation of the soul.

The hermeticist knows about such things, and for him this is the inner alchemy, as already mentioned.

Because the study and practice of hermetics is an integral part of a hermeticist's life, like the *refinement of their own soul*, and is continued throughout their life.

The hermetic seal of light consists of a circle, triangle and square. The basic shapes of *sacred* geometry. This already symbolises internalisation!

Among other things, it symbolises the soul, the spirit and the body. These three elements form the inner alchemical transformation, whereby each element is in equilibrium with the others.

It also contains the three levels of hermetic philosophy.

The great physical level.

The great spiritual level.

The great purely spiritual level.

You will find this hermetic **seal of light** on every page described. It not only serves as a reminder and preservation, but also as an anchor through all times.

The *Hermetic Seal of Light* is also used by Hermeticists to establish a connection to the elements through meditation, in relation to the 7 principles.

As a **tip,** I would like to add here to visualise this seal with closed eyes, to create it according to your inner inspiration and desire, in the corresponding colour (vibration) that is desired.

It is also used as a protective symbol to ward off negative energies and attract or transform positive energy - negative into positive!

This is an alchemical process!

This *tool* is elementary to understand!

In the hermetic tradition and teachings, the hermetic seal of light is therefore also regarded as a *tool* for *spiritual transformation*.

By applying the hermetic principles and harmonising their energies, we will achieve a spiritual development and a connection to the universe that we will gradually deepen.

In the symbolism of the Seal of Light, much knowledge is hidden - hermetically sealed, through all levels of being. The symbols themselves can also be seen as numbers. Those who calculate with the numbers will find interesting things.

A key to further understanding hermeticism. Here, a deeper exploration is only necessary if it is self-examined!

This decision is up to each individual, but I also see this as a worthwhile endeavour.

Let's start by placing our understanding, trust and gratitude in the seven principles/keys of hermetics.

This dedication is very rewarding for our spiritual path in life.

"The keys of Hermeticism are like rays of

knowledge from the eternal flame of wisdom"

Hermetic philosophy

The Principle the Spirituality

A conscious mind determines his path in life.

The universe is spirit, the universe is spiritual.

Kybalion

The universe is spiritual - held in the spirit of the universe.

Kybalion

The principle of spirituality

It is not a misprint that the two sayings from the Kybalion are directly below each other. They illustrate the principle of spirituality very well.

This principle is considered the most fundamental law of the 7 Principles of Hermeticism.

It is clearly and simply defined.

Everything consists of consciousness.

Everything has arisen from consciousness.

Everything is sustained by consciousness.

Our mind is both a transmitter and a receiver. Let's make use of this now!

The internalisation of spirituality comes gradually and becomes more consistent and clearer. Meditation and philosophising about hermetics are a good guide for this.

Anchors" can also be used, e.g. sticking small notes on mirrors and fridges.

Affirmation

Guide your inner thoughts; so the outer reality will follow.

Example:

I call careless thoughts the *Charly Braun effect*. If someone is constantly caught up in their negative thoughts, their head becomes heavy and falls forwards as they walk.

It is important to use the mind/thought as a tool. We are *pure* consciousness!

Just by repeatedly saying positive sentences, we can improve our

consciousness/mind in a very positive way and change our reality accordingly.

The same applies to negative beliefs in the other direction.

Example:

"I'm getting better and better every day in every respect!"

Emile Couè

We exist independently of our thoughts - we are pure consciousness! If we understand how to guide our thoughts through concentration and mindful thinking, many doors and new possibilities open up for our path in life.

In the emptiness of thought is the flame of wisdom and happiness!

Exercise: Concentration of thoughts

Imagine any object, the more precise the better. Hold it in your mind, if another thought comes into your consciousness, increase your concentration on your object.

Initially it will be seconds, later the time will increase.

This exercise is therefore so important, if you want to send something, a good amplifier is advisable.

The same applies to the receiver within us. It should be tuned to many frequencies in order to be in the necessary resonance.

Exercise: Emptiness of thoughts

Create a thought void! Initially, many thoughts will drift into your consciousness. Everyday life, things that still need to be done, appointments, dates, etc.

Imagine yourself as a silent observer, watching which thoughts flow in. The less energised thoughts can be removed from your consciousness quite quickly.

Those with more energy, i.e. the stubborn thoughts, can be removed by not paying attention to them (suppression).

Because such thoughts consume more energy to maintain.

Once a certain level of skill has been achieved in these two exercises, we can set our sights on our actual goal. Of course, it is up to each individual to decide how to assess their own skill. We have to learn to give our conscious thoughts more strength, energy and willpower. At the same time, we need to deprive the unwanted thoughts of the same.

Thoughts are a tool. We are not the tool, but the one who knows how to use it.

The parable of the two wolves:

Two wolves are fighting in your heart, one good and one bad. Which wolf will win? The wolf that is fed the most will be the one that grows.

With this reinforcement you set your thought, wish, idea or intention in motion: from the inside to the outside, so that it also gets back from the outside to the inside!

In between, switch to receiver, i.e. create a thought void and observe what you receive.

TIP:

Take your time, good things take time!

Notes:

This page is for your thoughts!

Notes:

This page is for your thoughts!

The Principle the Correspondence

All being has its equivalent on all levels.

As above, so below, as below, so above.

Kybalion

The principle of correspondence

The harmony that underlies this principle is the truth about the secrets of the nature of the universe.

This principle permeates all levels and is considered a *universal* law.

In a simple division, the material (gross material), spiritual (subtle2) and pure spiritual level (original source, God, Eli). Studying the levels is very rewarding work and offers deeper insights.

This principle is an important spiritual and mental tool for our life's journey.

Tip:

Meditating on this principle helps!

Affirmation

The inner spiritual and mental world is reflected in the outer world.

Example:

Let's resolve to look out for red cars today! As a result, more red-coloured cars will appear in our consciousness.

The inner attitude is reflected on the outside. It is therefore an absolute necessity to pay attention to your thoughts and also to cultivate them, which is a very important aspect.

If you change your thought forms and pathways, such as negative beliefs, then it will change on the outside, like a self-fulfilling prophecy.

Some of these paths have become motorways through time and the energy of thought.

It is therefore often only possible to fill these pathways with new and different thoughts, with energy, in order to change them.

This new direction of thought flow should then also be considered over a longer full stop of time.

The principle of correspondence will unfold according to the given law.

A practical example of the principle of correspondence is the interplay between our physical body and our mental state: when we feel stressed and unwell, this often manifests itself in the form of physical symptoms such as headaches or stomach aches.

On the other hand, physical illnesses can also affect our mental state and burden us emotionally with feelings.

This shows us that there is a correspondence between our mental and physical state.

A good example of the principle of correspondence is our relationship between our thoughts and our outer life.

When we have negative thoughts and focus on what we don't have, these thoughts often manifest in the form of difficulties and challenges in our lives (Charly Braun effect). However, when we focus on positive thoughts and opportunities, these thoughts often manifest in the form of success and happiness.

According to the principle of correspondence, we must be aware that there is a correspondence, an exchange between different levels of the universe,

that our thoughts and behaviour have an impact on all levels.

Exercise: Shifting your thoughts

By focussing on positive thoughts and actions, we can manifest the results we want and create the life path we desire.

The universe does not judge!

Good self-reflection is necessary in order to become aware of how our thoughts and actions influence our reality. We often see ourselves and our environment in a distorted mirror that does not correspond to the true reality. It is very important to recognise ourselves and look at ourselves with honesty. Then the distorting mirror loses its power and we can make the necessary adjustments to achieve positive results.

This principle also states that there is a connection between the microcosm of the individual, our being and the macrocosm of the universe.

At every level of **existence** there are correspondences that help us to understand the nature of the universe.

Astrology is a good example of this principle. Seeing the movements of the celestial bodies/energies and their position, e.g. at our birth, has an influence on our entire being.

The frequencies and vibrations that flow through us at this moment characterise us.

Science and our natural observations have shown us that patterns and structures that can be seen on a small scale are also repeated on a larger scale. For example, the shape of a branch resembles a river system, or a mountain range resembles tree roots. The shapes of a galaxy, for example, resemble a whirlwind or a whirlpool in the water. There are lots of them.

This concept of mirroring shows that everything in the universe is connected and is the same on a simple and deeper level.

Here, too, it takes a certain amount of practice and time to get our thoughts and ideas back on track.

The more often we remind ourselves of this, the easier and simpler it will be for us and the desired success will materialise.

Tip:

Combine the wish, idea or concept with a matching feeling!

Notes:

This page is for your thoughts!

Notes:

This page is for your thoughts!

Notes:

This page is for your thoughts!

The Principle the Vibration

Everything is in motion, nothing is at rest.

Nothing is at rest, everything is in motion, everything is vibration.

Kybalion

The principle of oscillation

The entire energy of the universe is in constant motion. These movements are frequencies, vibrations and oscillations throughout all levels.

Affirmation

Nothing is at rest, everything is in motion, everything is oscillating and vibrating.

The art of applying this principle for us lies in its simplicity.

Example:

Our aim is to increase the inner frequency, i.e. the number of vibrations.

There is no shortage, everything is available in abundance!

Impregnating a wish with a new thought and feeling takes place in real time!

This means imagining the fulfilment of the wish in such a way that it already exists.

This gradually becomes easier and faster through repeated practice (performance).

The principle of vibration is an important principle of hermetic philosophy. It states that everything in the universe is in motion and has a certain frequency or vibration. This vibration can exist on different levels, including physical, emotional and spiritual vibrations.

A practical example of the principle of vibration is music. Every sound has a certain frequency and vibration that can affect a person's emotions and mood.

For example, slow, relaxing music can have a calming effect, while fast, energising music can have a stimulating effect. There are music therapy programmes that aim to use the vibrations of music to help people treat anxiety, depression and other emotional problems.

Another example is the vibration of thoughts and emotions. Every thought and emotion has a certain frequency and vibration that can radiate to our environment and others around us. When we have positive and loving thoughts, we can create a positive vibration that can affect us and others around us.

Conversely, negative thoughts and emotions can create a negative vibration and separate us from others and our higher self, i.e. our consciousness.

The principle of vibration can also be applied to nature.

Everything in nature vibrates at a certain frequency, from the movement of stars/energy in the universe to the vibration of atoms and molecules.

These influences can also be applied to the seasons, as each period has a certain vibration and energy.

Likewise, time itself contains different qualities that we can strengthen or weaken as required.

Overall, the principle of vibration shows that everything in the universe is in motion and has a certain frequency or vibration.

It can be applied to many aspects of life and helps us to connect with our surroundings and become aware of how we can influence our own vibration.

We need to be mindful of the vibrations we send out and receive!

This controlled thought work is very important, it strengthens our spirit, our mental power and gives us back self-confidence and self-responsibility!

This is a very important aspect of our life's journey!

Through these application principles, we can learn how to influence our vibrations in a positive way and evolve on our spiritual path.

"He who understands the principle of vibration has seized the sceptre of power"

An old master.

Notes:

This page is for your thoughts!

Notes:

This page is for your thoughts!

Notes:

This page is for your thoughts!

The Principle the Polarity

Everything is twofold; everything has two poles.

Everything is twofold, everything has two poles, everything has its pair of opposites; equal and unequal are the same; opposites are identical in nature, only different in degree; extremes touch each other; all truths are only half truths; all contradictions can be harmonised with each other.

Kybalion

The principle of polarity

The supposed opposites, such as good and evil, or light and shadow, form two opposite poles.

It can be seen as a coin with two sides. It is a coin with different ways of looking at it.

Example:

The coin has the symbol on one side and a number on the other. No matter how we turn and look at the coin, it remains the same coin, neither the value of the coin changes nor its appearance. Only our point of view favours one side of the coin or the other.

We have certainly all experienced the vibrations of hate or love and the rapid changes that can occur.

The emotions are spinning in their poles and we experience a real rollercoaster ride.

Only when we sort out or control our thoughts again do we gradually regain inner peace.

We have to learn and practise paying attention to our thoughts and feelings!

An example from nature shows us this polarity in day and night. Day and night are opposite poles, but they are inextricably linked. Every day has a night and every night has a day. Day and night are interdependent and complement each other to form a complete cycle.

A spiritual and mental example is the concept of love and hate. Love and hate are opposite poles, but they are inextricably linked, like a coin. Without the experience of hate, we would not be able to appreciate and understand the beauty and joy of love.

Without love, hate could influence us very negatively, without hate, love could influence us very positively.

Polarities can be set like a slider in one direction or the other from the neutrality of the centre.

Where there is love, there is no room for hate and vice versa!

Water is a polar substance!

Water has two poles - one positive and one negative - they are also inextricably linked. We can imprint water with information, or use water to purify negative elements. We can easily see this if we understand water as a solvent and binding agent. Many chemical (alchemy) reactions make life on our planet as we know it possible in the first place.

Overall, the principle of polarity shows that everything in the universe has two opposing poles that are inextricably linked.

Exercise: Reinforcement!

Both poles are necessary, but we can strengthen the positive aspects and reduce the negative aspects. Thought work is also necessary here and the focus is on concentrating our thoughts, directing them towards one pole or the other in order to negate the other pole.

These poles are interdependent and complement each other to form a complete cycle. By understanding and applying this principle, we can learn how to balance and harmonise the forces in life in order to live a complete and fulfilling life.

I think that you, dear reader, will gain an understanding that hermetics and its applications are a way of life that achieves its effect through internalisation.

Tip:

Constant repetition and meditation make our endeavours much easier!

Affination:

> Our actions are becoming more responsible!

Notes:

This page is for your thoughts!

Notes:

This page is for your thoughts!

Notes:

This page is for your thoughts!

The Principle of the Rhythm

The rhythm swings from pole to pole.

Everything flows in and out, everything has its tides, all things rise and fall, the swinging of the pendulum is evident in everything; the measure of the swing to the right is the measure of the swing to the left; rhythm compensates.

Kybalion

The principle of rhythm

The rhythm creates a perpetual cycle, also through all levels of the universe, and is connected to polarity.

Neutralisation is used to counteract the principle or to move it in one direction or the other.

Example:

This principle cannot be avoided, but the effect can be changed to a certain extent for oneself and also for others.

This rhythm can be influenced by conscious thinking.

Exercise: Neutralisation!

The transfer of feelings and emotions into the oppositeness of the stronger momentum reduces the swings of the rhythm.

Here too, repeated practice and analysing the effect is fundamental!

When the simplicity of this principle is internalised, clarity about this law is gained.

Another example is our body's breathing cycle, which not only connects us to other levels, but also follows a rhythm of inhaling and exhaling with a short pause in between.

This rhythm is crucial for the absorption of oxygen and the exchange of carbon dioxide in our material body. The spiritual body is maintained by the subtle substance of the breath.

The breathing cycle also shows that everything in the body follows a certain rhythm, which is important for the functioning and maintenance of our body and mind.

The principle of rhythm also applies to human relationships. Relationships often have phases of growth, crisis, renewal and stagnation, but also of love!

Understanding this rhythm can help to strengthen and improve relationships by paying attention to which phase they are going through and how best to adapt to it for yourself and your partner.

Overall, the principle of rhythm states that everything in the universe follows a certain rhythm and a certain cycle.

This principle can help us to become more aware of the fact that life runs in cycles and that there are phases of development and rest. As already mentioned, these different qualities can also be found in time.

If we understand and apply this principle, we can better harmonise our lives with the natural rhythms of the universe.

Notes:

This page is for your thoughts!

Notes:

This page is for your thoughts!

The Principle from Cause & effect

Every cause has its effect and vice versa.

Every cause has its effect, every effect its cause, everything happens according to law, coincidence is just the name for an unknown law. There are many levels of causality, but nothing escapes the law.

Kybalion

The principle of cause & effect

By shifting one's own mind to a higher level and degree of density, the cause will become the effect. It is easy to understand in an example.

Example:

You change a situation by switching from "reacting" to "acting". In order to achieve success, it is important that we move to a level that corresponds to the desired change.

If possible, we should always reach the level above in order to recognise what the effect is in the situation.

This puts us in a position to change the course of our lives, so that we gradually become more of an involved *player* and not just an unwilling *pawn!*

Affirmation:

We are not the *character*, we are the **player!**

An actor is not the character he plays! He plays the **role** of the character.

Imagine *Jonny* Deep playing the role of *Captain Jack Sparrow*, then leaving the set in costume after filming his scene and staying in character. Everyone would think he was crazy and he himself wouldn't see or understand his own reality!

When we lose ourselves in the role of the actor, we lose control over ourselves and our surroundings, reality and our path in life.

We also become **more agile** by practising and learning how to deal with a situation that we want to change.

A good example of the principle of cause and effect is the way we look after our health.

If we have an unhealthy diet and do little physical activity, the cause of these choices is our lifestyle. The effect of this can be that we are more susceptible to illness and feel unwell overall. The inner radiance is shown on the outside, both physically and mentally.

However, if we take care of our health and eat a healthy diet, exercise regularly or similar, the cause of our decisions is a healthy lifestyle. The effect will be that we feel better overall and fall ill less often.

Let's take a closer look at interpersonal relationships.

I think this is a very important point in our lives, because we usually want to have a loved one, a good soul by our side.

When we are kind and respectful to others, the cause is our behaviour; the effect is that we will build positive relationships with others and make more friends. Love enters our stage, so to speak!

However, if we act inappropriately or treat others disrespectfully, the cause of such actions may be a lack of self-control or a lack of empathy, and the effect will be that we damage relationships or isolate ourselves.

In both negative cases, it is certainly not beneficial for our soul and spirit.

Overall, the principle of cause and effect shows us that everything we do has consequences (karma). When we are aware that every action has a cause and effect, we can better focus on making positive choices to create a positive impact in our environment.

Understanding this principle can also help us to achieve our goals and ambitions by focussing on the causes that are necessary to achieve the effects we want.

This exercise is fundamental!

Notes:

This page is for your thoughts!

Notes:

This page is for your thoughts!

Notes:

This page is for your thoughts!

The Principle Of the sex

Ying and yang are always present.

Gender is in everything, everything has male and female principles, gender manifests itself on all levels.

Kybalion

The principle of gender

is a principle of creation, of witness and maintains the cycle of life.

If both parts of gender are understood and the principle is internalised, we come into our creative power or energy.

In this way, we influence our life path into a creative action. This can then be used to initiate or strengthen creative processes.

Example:

Creative processes in particular experience an enormous power of creation as a result. A painter, sculptor, writer etc. utilises this energy specifically for their works.

The creative power combined with the law of cause and effect changes his life path. In general, the principle of gender is a necessity for creative projects of all kinds!

All laws are interconnected, interwoven through all levels.

The clearer the insight and understanding of these 7 principles is gained, the more we can move forward on our self-determined path in life.

Example:

The way we approach creative projects.

All creative work requires a masculine energy to conceive ideas and a feminine energy to absorb and realise these ideas.

The masculine energy is the initial impulse or idea that is born and the feminine energy is the art and way in which this idea is realised.

Both in harmony promise positive results!

Another example of the principle of gender is the relationship between the body and the mind. The body could be considered a masculine energy as it acts and influences the physical world, while the mind could be considered a feminine energy as it provides the thoughts that underlie actions.

The principle of gender can also be applied in spirituality.

The masculine energy can be seen as the conscious self that can actively act and make decisions, while the feminine energy can be seen as the subconscious, the spiritual side. Overall, the principle of gender shows that all forces in nature exist in a duality of male and female energy and that these energies are in constant exchange and balance with each other.

Exercise: Mind connection!

Through a deeper understanding of this principle, we can create *balance* in our lives by consciously focusing on integrating both masculine and feminine energy in our decisions and actions.

If both parts are included in our decisions, the resulting actions will always be in harmony!

If we look at a decision from many different angles, viewed as a whole according to the hermetic principles, we are certainly right!

Notes:

This page is for your thoughts!

Considerations!

Understanding and acting according to the seven principles of hermeticism is certainly a task that must be carried out with all due care.

But the more we unlock the secrets of hermetics, the more we will benefit from it.

Because true change takes place within each individual! On a small and large scale.

If many people were to experience an inner positive change, a greater positive change could be seen and understood as a whole; this would work through all physical levels as well as through all spiritual levels. Immersing yourself in your own spirit is truly a fantastic journey into yourself.

Personally, I am always fascinated by recognising new facets of myself.

The wide range of different degrees of consciousness is immeasurable!

Simply put:

It is the eternal and infinite consciousness, we ourselves!

Once you realise this fact, there is no longer any impossibility. Of course, this is a long process. As it says in the Star Wars Tm series

The Mandolarin the apt phrase:

This is the way!

Surely each of us has a different starting point on this path. We meet companions and new and old friends. We are not alone. Yes - some only accompany you for a certain amount of time, not everyone follows the same path.

Sometimes we lose our way ourselves, that is also part of it. It is important to find this path again, and there are also helpful hands to help us do this.

Another time we will return this helping hand!

I myself will also use this book like a workbook, enter notes and continue my soul mirror here. This is not a book for the bookshelf, use it!

Tip: you can add a date to one or other of the notes. Also use the space under the *seal of light* to make a note.

I like to use writing cards in all my books as bookmarks to record my thoughts.

I would like to add something to my recommendations and considerations:

My experience in harmonising soul, mind and body.

Comparable to a jigsaw puzzle, part by part the picture becomes clearer and clearer!

In addition to the *hermetic* exercises, I have also started quantum meditation, so I can't give an exact value yet. The fact is that I feel better. This aspect alone shows the value of continuing to practise it.

Of course, everyone who starts with practical applications of hermetics will gain their own experiences and insights, according to their **individuality**.

Finally, you will find space for your highly personalised soul mirror. This is intended **only** for you, where you can carry out your soul refinement according to the 7 principles of hermeticism.

Without soul refinement or character training, the true spiritual path is closed!

Be honest with yourself!

Write down your negative and positive characteristics and decipher them, for example according to the elements and the seven principles. Strengthen one or other positive quality and weaken or remove your negative qualities.

Many people see themselves in a distorted mirror, as mentioned before, and the true reality is obscured. Recognising yourself is essential!

By understanding the basics of hermetics, you can then bring reality into the flow of your choice. Either to maintain it or to weaken or strengthen it as the case may be.

Transforming negative qualities/energies into positive ones is our alchemical process!

This is hermetic alchemy!

The more cogwheels mesh like clockwork and are attuned to each other in harmonious motion, the more we too will tune into the harmony of the universe.

The light of wisdom protects,

protects and carries us all!

A seer

Notes:

This page is for your thoughts!

Conclusion and closing remarks

What conclusion do the 7 principles of hermetics in this book offer us?

First of all, knowledge of the 7 principles of hermetics. Of course, these can also be found in other books on Hermeticism, but it is the foundation.

By understanding the principles, we can learn to better understand our life path and ourselves. Our actions are determined by our understanding. Remember the quote from Buddha.

It is the flame of wisdom!

It is not the will that drives our actions, but the imagination.

Coué

In my opinion, a greater gift than the *flame of wisdom* is hardly possible for a spiritual consciousness. It shifts our spirit and gives good souls a foothold in all times!

I am extremely grateful and fully appreciate this knowledge!

This universal bunch of keys, with seven keys, opens up areas within ourselves that would not be possible without this knowledge. Let us use it wisely and with caution.

It reveals to us the order of all being.

Figuratively speaking: A magician who is constantly discovering new areas and rooms in his magical tower. The level/image changes as you play!

A magician only leaves his tower when external circumstances require it.

The study of hermetics is certainly seen and understood over a longer period of time. But when we understand, really understand, that we are *infinite* and *eternal* **consciousness**, time no longer plays any role at all!

I would like to thank you for accompanying my thoughts and for reading my texts in this book. I am very pleased if I have been able to contribute something useful to you, dear readers, in understandable words for your spiritual journey through life.

"I wish you all a familiar light for your steps on all your paths."

In the *list of sources* you will find other books that can support you on your spiritual path.

To our question at the beginning of the book:

*But how do these laws come about that ultimately gave rise to our **universe** and thus to all of **existence**?*

Only the original source is not subject to the 7 principles of hermeticism. This is because it is on its own level.

"The great, purely spiritual level"

It radiates the 7 principles of hermetics from within itself (seven-rayed star). Each principle of hermetics represents a corner of the star and its ray of light. The constant flow of energies is able to create the universe, and the infinite flow sustains it.

The original source determines the laws of the principles.

It is therefore not subject to the laws of Hermeticism. It is the **originator** and **keeper** of the *hermetic* laws and principles!

I would like to add one last sentence at the end. I have internalised this sentence through studying hermetics/magic over the course of time, and it applies to me.

It is not about the absolute truth, firstly it depends on the degree of realisation and secondly it describes the path that one is prepared to take - **the path of truth.**

This path changes life. It is the inner transformation of the soul that brings this about. The gift for this is:

Recognise yourself!

In the Tarot deck, this book corresponds to the fourth card. The **Ruler!**

According to the **principle** of **correspondence**.

With best thoughts and wishes for your spiritual journey through life, Chris.

"Who knows the truth,

is destined to change his life.

That is the price"

C. A. M. W.

END

Soul refinement

Soul refinement

Soul refinement

Soul refinement

Soul refinement

Soul refinement

Soul refinement

List of sources

Three Initiates, William Walker Arkinson

Kybalion - The 7th Hermetic Laws. The original.

20th edition

ISBN 978-3-937392-17-2

Franz Bardon

The path to becoming a true adept

19th edition Wuppertal 2001

ISBN 3-921338-30-1

W.E. Butler

The high school of magic

4th edition 1989

ISBN 3-7626-0317-0

Dr Michael König

The small quantum temple

3rd edition 2011

ISBN 978-3-942166-21-8

Emile Coué

Autosuggestion

2nd edition, 2014

ISBN 978-3-03800-682-4

Coué

Self-mastery

through conscious autosuggestion

German by Dr Paul Amann

121,000-150,000

Benno Schwabe & Co, publisher. Basel 1926

Milton Keynes UK
Ingram Content Group UK Ltd.
UKHW022119021224
451693UK00023B/1181

9 783769 308082